PRAISE FOR *Approaching the Gate*

"The ghosts of fairy tales live in these pages and color their deceptively simple surfaces, as Lynette Reini-Grandell artfully blends meditation, history, and the risk inherent in love into poetic form. The fundament of these poems is the earth that nurtures and buries us, that supports farms and horses and trees and fire and wine. As in fairy tale, it is the generosity of human spirit in the face of difficulties that tentatively and momentarily and brightly distinguishes us. The pleasures that await the reader of this volume are physical, unsparing, and profound."

—Sidney Wade, author of *Straits & Narrows: Poems*

"*Approaching the Gate* is ganged with love and its many conflicting faces and bodies—human, celestial, animal. Love is the subject of this book— love's difficulties, and dreams and longing to be unburdened of the beauty of life dreaming its many faces, bodies, and days—all the while, in love with even love's impossibility, without which there (as the poet illuminates) can be no miracles. I love this debut book full of miracles where 'even the vegetables sing'."

—Ed Bok Lee, author of *Whorled*

"In Lynette Reini-Grandell's new collection of poems she writes in the title poem: 'Pull apart anything that covers/scrape away whatever doesn't fit.' The truth is, everything in this beautiful collection fits. We would feel the loss if any single poem suddenly vanished. In this book there's room for love, discord, sorrow, history, loneliness, transformation, the sensuous, horses exactly as themselves, and as guides of the spirit, nature, and all its creatures, surprising leaps of image and intention—a bounty. The poet asks, 'Will there ever be/another world/like this one?' No, not really. This is Lynette Reini-Grandell's world, and we are fortunate to live it inside these poems of hers. In the first poem of this collection, the poet writes, 'I can drive, let me do this much./Let me watch the road.' Yes. Let her drive, and watch the world for us."

—Deborah Keenan,

author of *From T* ... *ld*

T0094515

APPROACHING THE GATE

POEMS BY LYNETTE REINI-GRANDELL

Holy Cow! Press :: Duluth, Minnesota :: 2014

First printing, 2014

ISBN 978-0-9859818-5-3

10 9 8 7 6 5 4 3 2

Grateful acknowledgment is made to the Minnesota State Arts Board for support with an
artist initiative grant in poetry and the Finlandia Foundation for supporting my investi-
gations into Finnish culture. Many thanks are also due my husband, Venus de Mars, who
kindly volunteered to paint what my mind's eye saw. I also want to thank members of
my writing group and mentors who gave loving feedback and encouragement when pre-
sented with earlier versions of these poems: Kris Bigalk, Todd Boss, Anthony Ceballos,
B.H. Fairchild, Deborah Keenan, Jules Nyquist, Marie Olofsdotter, Matt Rasmussen,
A.E. Stallings, Scott Vetsch, Sidney Wade, Paulette Warren, and Susan Zeni.

This project is supported in part by grant awards from the Ben and Jeanne Overman
Charitable Trust, the Elmer L. and Eleanor J. Andersen Foundation, the Cy and Paula
DeCosse Fund of the Minneapolis Foundation, The Lenfestey Family Foundation, and
by gifts from individual donors.

Holy Cow! Press books are distributed to the trade by Consortium Book Sales &
Distribution, c/o Perseus Distribution, 210 American Drive, Jackson, TN 38301.

For inquiries, please write to:
Holy Cow! Press, Post Office Box 3170, Mount Royal Station, Duluth, MN 55803.

Visit *www.holycowpress.org*

Acknowledgments

"Approaching the Gate" appeared in *TRIVIA: Voices of Feminism*, issue 15, Fall, 2013.

"The Dandelion Gatherer" appeared in *The River Muse*, March, 2013.

"Fix My Shoes" appeared in the Fall, 2013 great weather for MEDIA anthology, *The Understanding between Foxes and Light*.

"Horses in Winter" appeared in *TRIVIA: Voices of Feminism*, issue 15, Fall, 2013.

"In Memory of Tennessee Williams, Who Died in 1983 after Choking on the Plastic Cap of a Pill Bottle" appeared in *Poetry City, USA 3*, 2013.

"Joe Dreamed He Was a Lithe, Brown Reptile" appeared in *Mo' Joe: The Anthology (The Continuing Saga of Joe the Poet, Vol. 2)* from Beatlick Press, 2014.

"My Husband with Long Hair" appeared in *Evergreen Chronicles* as part of the performance-art script, "Dearly Beloved," Fall, 1996.

"The Naturalist" appeared in *The Centrifugal Eye*, Autumn, 2013.

"Our Queer Marriage" appeared in *Evergreen Chronicles* in slightly different form as part of the performance-art script, "Dearly Beloved," Fall, 1996.

"Radio Girls" appeared in the great weather for MEDIA anthology, *It's Animal but Merciful*, Fall, 2012.

"Still Life" appeared in slightly different form in *Poetry Motel*, issue 3, March, 1985.

"The Thoroughbred's Black Knees" appeared in slightly different form in *Poetry City, USA 2*, 2012.

"This Horse's Ears" appeared on MNArtists.org as a What Light poetry winner, 2010.

"Through the Ice" appeared in *Revolver*, Fall 2013.

"To Change the World" appeared in *Prøof Magazine*, Volume 1, Issue 3, Summer, 2014.

Contents

I

II

III

For Bug

As We Drove

1

As we drove we talked about the stars,
how gravity, the universe
exerting all its pull at the moment
of emergence from an amniotic sea,
sent us screaming in our own peculiar
spirals.

Dust that once was stars and now is human
pulls your blood and psyche one way, headlong,
makes your one true love the worst companion
possible.

        Atomic weight of stars, planets,
black holes, all matter, flotsam, jetsam,
spins two souls in opposite directions,
shouting I love you, I love you, I can
no longer stand to be near you.

2

The universe looks down on this, dumbly
or with consciousness, take your pick.

I, your witness, keep on driving, hands
on wheel, eyes fixed to the road.

Something sends you dreams you can't ignore.

In one, San Francisco shudders with an earthquake,
and two weeks later the double-decker bridge
collapses on itself, just like in your vision.

Now the little girl you love is crying
in your dream; you wake and hope
that you can help her, but you don't know, no one
knows.

3

No one knows who sends us dreams:
spirits in the clouds, or sad ghosts like
the suicidal ghost your mother saw
in the center of her room.

Save your eyes for tracing constellations,
listen to the wheels hum.

I can drive, let me do this much.
Let me watch the road.

MY HUSBAND WITH LONG HAIR

No mirror, but a deep, reflecting pool,
you are uncanny, destabilizing,
like a twin, but your hair grows much faster.
It is a gleaming, red mahogany,
hair that lengthens, sways from side to side.

And I love your hips; they are just
what I have always wanted. You have gorgeous,
slender fingers, cool to touch.
                              Dear slender
stem, I know you could be fragile. And if
you are fragile, who will come protect me?
If you are shy, then who will stand to save me?
If you are ravishing, then who will wish
to ravish me?
                    I drop these stones, one
by one, into dark, mysterious water,
watch them sink. The image is distorted.
You are not my twin. I see you creeping
at the edge, like a lion or
a panther come to drink from this cool water.

I slip beside and cling to your smooth shoulder.

In That Country

All the windows
open to the sea.

Water laves
the kelp-drenched rocks.

The gray-green ocean rolls and swells
like muscles of a giant man.

Sun so bright, air so cold,
taste of salt on lips—

I long to see you smile again
when you say my name.

New York, Carlton Arms Art Hotel

One city-hot summer, we slept with windows open,
a sculpture studying our every toss and turn.

It was a woman, eyes wide, mouth open,
electric red light inside: glowing, aroused,
deranged: her panting mouth our urgent night light.

And on the wall a painted man, angst-ridden,
crept up his cubist staircase, eyes cast down,
in tones of gray and black and cold, cold red,
coagulate cold color of stilled blood.

I tried to lure you to the fire escape
with wine, two plastic glasses, a large ashtray.
You felt uncomfortable, could not stay long;
I could not go back into that room.

You had your way of coping—it mirrored, maybe,
how you felt: hot, cold, scarlet,
then a dreary gray.

Did you remember to take your pills today?

I saw you were at home in the room from hell,
so I walked down Third Avenue, admiring
fruits and flowers, all beautiful things to buy;
I dipped into my wallet for a drink.

On our hotel's landing, there is also
a plate of money placed in front of Buddha:
a plate of money, it would taste so good.

STILL LIFE

1

A woman in a red dress pales
under the green glare
of an all-night diner.
She pushes her coffee cup away
and stares into
her hand, avoids looking
at the man sitting next to her.
Her other hand
nearly touches his.

2

Later
naked, she reclines stiffly
on elbows,
eyes wide
open.

3

To make her beautiful
you might
imagine the citrine light
falling through
her hair,
add a line of vivid blue
along the curve of her cheek.

4

You would watch leaves
falling in the orchard
and brighten
the edge
of an apple
after dark.

RADIO GIRLS

Radio girls want to fall asleep with someone singing in their ears;
Radio girls all developed huge crushes on David Bowie and some
     never got over it.
Radio girls are nearly inconsolable.
Radio girls would rather go blind than remove their ear buds.
Radio girls say,
Dream-crusher, what have you done for me lately?

Radio girls shout syllables rapidly into microphones shocking
     their lips and channeling Patti Smith,
Radio girls have dark circles under their eyes but it might
     be from smeared mascara.
Radio girls sit on the curb and scowl because they are too shy
     to start conversations,
Radio girls need to get off their asses and finish that novel
     about the yellow brick road.

Radio girls are on a road which is uncharted—
Radio girls work with deliberate care to arrange the right soundtrack
     that will follow them everywhere.
Radio girls do not have free hearts,
they are leashed to their hearts,
and when they see their hearts walking up the sidewalk,
one of them turns sideways
under the overhang
and closes the door
without looking back once.

THE WINE IN THIS GLASS

is darker than lipstick—
it breaches the rim,
it sloshes the edge,
it dribbles on my knuckles.
I suck the juice off my index finger,
press it again to the glass
to hold back the flood.

I am contemplating love and risk,
a wall going up around Palestine,
me and you.
I wish I had read John Locke
a long time ago when I had the chance—
philosophy seemed like too much work.
My fingers are wet and sticky:
another swallow of wine
makes the red tide recede.

I'm a yeller and a shouter
but my empty kitchen
is only good for a metal stove and dark thoughts.
Why do you think crows only travel in threes?
I just saw twenty dart across the darkening sky.
You unsettle me.
Forgive me,
I am unsteady,
I spill.

APPROACHING THE GATE

Peel back the feathers, peel back the fur.
The pale, protective skin—peel that away too.

Pull apart anything that covers,
scrape away whatever doesn't fit.

Let light stream in at the speed of blood,
slice past cornea, sclera, iris, retina.

Anything to fell the green-leaved past
and pave a roadway,

anything to get to the inside,
anything to plow this ground under.

OUR QUEER MARRIAGE

Some images: a fine romantic dinner,
the waiter asks us what we "ladies" want.
You do not correct him.

Or you're standing at the stove:
I introduce a friend.
She cannot comprehend that the person
there before her is named Steve, and I
cannot comprehend her own confusion.

Was I so out of touch?
Touch is what I need to bring me back,
but the public lens of paranoia
makes you fear to take my hand: what if
you are passing as a woman? What
will they think of us?

When our friends were not allowed to marry,
you asked me to divorce symbolically—
a goodwill gesture, just a piece of paper;
when the dust had settled, point achieved,
we'd marry once again.

I thought we were a ship
that steered between the rocks:
now I'm freezing from the icy deeps.
I ask you,
take my hand.

Joe Dreamed He Was a Lithe, Brown Reptile

drowsing deep in Mississippi silt and duckweed,
head aimed south, beard flowing with the eddies,
tail snaked north toward Minnesota tributaries,
humming as the waters coursed his scales
like glaciers letting go their weight in water,
each rivulet a gentle, muddy trace,
each rhythmic curl a memory of smoke:
he turned and lightly snagged the coffee surface,
stretched out his unsheathed, sodden paw,
and touched the current of the other sleeping beast.

WOODEN PUPPET BOY

I miss those days when your cool, smooth-grained hand held mine,
you were real to me then.

Descended from a talking tree,
you knew slow growth of green sap through your veins,
communed with birds, cats, foxes, stag-horn beetles, crickets,
fought with monsters, floated out to sea, lived inside a fish,
befriended those who had no other friends.
The villagers agreed there were special properties to wood.

Do you remember how it felt to be a living beast of burden,
your donkey skin stretched tight into a drum?
You survived it all, a miracle,
that was real, too.

The other kind of real is
I liked you better before you became a human boy,
before time turned into an enemy,
before six pills a day, one for heart,
two for blood,
three to forget what you have lost.

I want to carve you out of wood again,
I want to hear you sing, I want
to see you dance
without the strings attached. I want
to hear your foolish promises again.

Who Rules Your Heart?

1

You could be ruled by beauty,
but who knows where that would lead—
oak trees, a crescendo, the hedges thick with blackberries.

Are your eyes drawn to the glow of sky overhead
between dark cottonwood branches
or the pale road,
glimpsed between the ears of a horse?

Have you stopped along the way?

Do you know who your mother is?

2

Something sets the moth in motion
to beat its wings against the breezes
or burn itself against the hot glass of a light bulb.
Something rules your heart,
something that must move.

The heart travels a narrow path.
The heart's eyes search the hills before it for light,
for its beacon,
beckoning,
calling.

On the mountain top the guiding fire
needs tending, coaxing,
someone to feed it.

Near that fire,
always,
the fire-tender's face and hands smudge with soot,
blacken by firelight,
and words change meanings.
The word for shining white—"bleak" or "blake"—
becomes black,
its necessary companion.

3

Who rules your heart?

Will you break your hand on someone's cheek?
Does it mean that much to you?

Do you listen when they cry to you?
Do you listen to the deep, deep sighs?

You might throw your heart over the fence,
you might leap ten times your stature into the air.
You might listen to singing.
You might open a book.
You might sit at the table and taste love's meat.

You might have courage.
You might continue.

ELEGY IN A TENNESSEE GRAVEYARD

1

Slow stones succumb to devouring mosses and lichens.
A thigh high mound lies beneath tall pines, a yellow
sand mass that measures time as it settles and drifts.

I go to the cemetery to think about poetry.

I don't miss the dead. I am missing the living, the aging,
all vibrant creatures.
                      I think of a small red horse.
When I call him out of his pasture, he whinnies, he gallops
towards me, ears forward, avid, an offer of grace.

He pushes my stomach hard with his nose,
testing friendship, attends the sound of my voice;
he watches where my gaze goes. It goes
to his generous eyes, brown river stones,

pupils like rectangles, scanning both sides of his world,
350 degrees, not directly in front,
not directly behind, he cannot see his own nose,
but he sees more than me.

I feed him.
I think of teeth, their sharp and expressive nature,
Something with tooth has a grip to hold onto,
teeth everlasting, like bones, useful for grazing.

He can move through a field, nose and mouth to the ground,
push past late summer goldenrod, barley grass, all gone
to seed. Teeth reveal age and molars wear down
with use.
                    Teeth might tally the men in this graveyard.

I'd know you, my love, from your teeth.
                                  You still haven't lost
your baby wolf incisor, childhood relic,
crowded to fit with your permanent teeth.
You're still trying to knit broken bones in your right fist.

The ossified bulge on the back of your hand remains
after we patched the punched wall, but this is no
memory of grief, this is something we shared,
we still share, we remember together.

3

The ground is uneven, spongy, maybe from moss
or earth perennially dug up and settled back down.
The land drops away on the other side of the wall
to green fecund forest, as good a place as any

for reverence, and lifting a huge body,
as no doubt one day I will have to do,
carry a body over a low boundary,
body of memory, body I do not want to forget.

At Night

At night we settled into our routine,
a glass of wine to make the meal, another
with the dinner to pretend the scene
romantic like a restaurant. But so much bother

went to cooking, cleaning that we never
talked. We never saw. Dreams deviled us;
we charged around the kitchen, hopes forever
scuttled, anger mounting, words tremendous,

a snap, and then the awkward notes of silence.
I sought out the piano, moody, fingered
each sad song, my signature defiance,
while you sat in your chair nearby, lingered

in the dark so your love could be felt.
You stayed with me. Snow at last does melt.

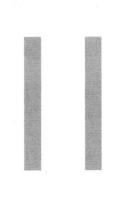

Wind

approaches an elm,
catches its western-most leaves.

Weather flows west to east,
through an invisible map,
boughs bounce back and forth,
twigs bend in counter-spring.

Larger limbs flex slowly in one direction,
branches toss in another.

Everything follows
a current, a trace.
Every tree
whorls from its stem.

The Naturalist

This small horse is a savvy naturalist,
a modern Linnaeus,
identifying then eschewing
violets, anemones,
preferring timothy
and first-growth clover.

It takes a four-footed expert
to draw attention
to apple trees blossoming
in the forest of a forgotten farmstead
where small spring leaves
do not hide the brighter blooms.
The naturalist moves past them now.
He will sense the apples later
when they have become round, ripe, and useful.

Last week the clover was not good enough,
only the succulent ligules of meadow-grass tasted right;
this week the palate expands,
dandelions gain a cunning astringency,
clover pre-bloom hints of sugar,
timothy's green honey flows through its fattening stem.

It's so clear how to live
when the head bows to the grass,
when one follows the contours of the curving world,
nuzzling all manner of insects in the soil
amid the year's yellowing roots.

He lifts his head occasionally
to see something in the distance,
a moving shadow,
the source of a strange new scent,
then stretches downward,
eagerly examining
the earth.

To Earth

Dirt feels the weight of someone's imprint,
grass knows it has been bent.
A cluster of sow-bugs beneath the concrete slab
listens to a slow march above them.

Grass struggles,
but it struggles in legion.
Beetles and worms know the walking world rests
on the labyrinths they build.

Dirt knows it is essential to everybody.

ORIGINS

My grandmother's mother's mother thought the world
started from an egg that rolled,
fell from a daughter's knee.

It did not hatch,
but separated into land and sky.
Its chips became the rocks;
its ooze became the waters.

It is still becoming,
swelling into shape.
It takes the form
sometimes of a bird,
sometimes of a woman's knee,
sometimes of a seed leaf,
rock, root, or shoot,
all that feeds the egg.

Everything becomes an egg or seed
to spawn the world,
before it catches in its talons,
falls between its feathers,
before it lodges in its biting beak.

Cows and Cowslips

Rusko is not a flower,
she is a light brown Guernsey cow
with gentle eyes, a pale pink nose,

and a white star upon her crown.
She eats green grass and hay
and gives warm milk and butter.

When I lean against her flank
and let her milk down
her hair smells like clover,

not like cowslips, creamy yellow flowers
cows devour in our pasture.
They won't eat buttercups.

Cows grow in pastures too.
They stand in bunches by the stream;
they dot the field like wildflowers,

and when the evening darkens
all the white stars shine upon their foreheads
as they amble on their Milky Way.

America Fever

The more he walked the land the more he loved it.
His sawyer crew would soon take all the white pines.
He could set the stumps with dynamite
to smooth the soil and, from behind a plow,

steer the strapping horses, "Gee," and "Ha."
He mailed two one-way tickets for the new world
to wife and daughter, built his farm. The dowser
said the water flowed clean underground.

On a farm with red clay soil, trees will grow—
a crop they chopped down, milled and squandered.
After that, scant pasture grows to feed
the cows that make it through the cold.

O land of wish and muscle, the north shore farm
was made of clay, could not sustain the dreams,
spring-fed, but not the fertile land he hoped for:
a country, not a friend, yet still a shelter.

Sugar

My hands dart hungrily
through kitchen cupboards
in search of some overlooked
sweet thing.

Someday
my bones will bleach white.

The two skeletons
of my intentions
and my demons
will settle
facing one another,
each curved inward in repose
at the edge of a remote field.

Maybe they will die in a fight,
maybe they will die
of the same poison,
two halves of a circle
falling towards each other,
green grass
growing taller,
taller
around my sugar
white
bones.

SONG OF THE DEAD CROW

Corn is a starchy vegetable,
full of sugar and heat;
its fruit grows on stalks and looks
nothing like a bird's ear.

There's no good reason for living,
but I am even more
disappointed in the view
from here.

My melody
doesn't sound much
like a bird's song,
either.

BEAR MARRIAGE

Do you take this honey-fond giant
as your celestial, starry-eyed spouse,

I do.

to have and to wrestle,
in clover and in coughing fits,

I do.

in frostbite and in warm milk
until villagers break into your drowsy den,

I do.

drag you from it,
and tenderly slaughter you

I do.

because you are cousins
and relations must help one another?

I do.

I now pronounce you all animals.

THRESHOLD OF DAWN

Seventeen horses gallop across a snowy gray pasture,
the bay with the white blaze leading,
nose lifted to ice-crystal air.
Horses spill across shadowed white drifts,
their sound carrying to me at my dark kitchen window.

Then the eye of the sun opens over the hill,
licking the frozen slopes with rose-gold rays.
Seventeen horses lift their heads higher, hooves roil the snow,
they launch out of their shadows,
they warm with light.

Wish Hounds

Cunning dogs
who bound and pour,
rapid through the underbrush—

their oblong bodies shine
like water streaming
through the land
so fast
it can't quench dirt.

I will scrape my avocation
clean away
to follow their dark surge,
their lilt,
to open with a cry.

Another name for wish hound
is the ghost
that lingers;
another name for linger
is to hunger.

Now is no time to pause
from hunger
to devour.

Wish hounds welter with the wind,
and on their every tongue they sing
a greedy hallelujah.

Soundings

A shining lake echoes with swimmers;
a yellow lab dives underwater,
disturbing silt, ragged tail
still visible, his joyous wet flag.

He chases fish.

In the soundtrack of an ideal relationship
two souls read, one on a couch,
one at a table, a parallel structure,
two notes sounding together.

They move downward then one holds,
waits, the other moves higher,
higher, major, tonic seventh,
unison waves.

The dog plunges in water, seeking
bright depths, speckled fish,
a cascading school of shimmering notes
swimming in chorus.

O soul,
if you touched your tongue to my center
what note would sound?

August Field

Say one day dry winds drove our heat-drenched hair
an image match for all our kindled thoughts,

say the air between your body and mine glowed,
grew heavy with hay-scent and twining wild grapes,

say I clasped your hand and led you to the blind edge
of a field where all our future rooted, budded, blossomed:

would you fall against me till we both could taste our hearts?
Would you open and breathe deep each wind-borne seed?

THE THOROUGHBRED'S BLACK KNEES

I open the gate
and shock to the touch of her swan-black neck.
She dips, she nuzzles, she forages,
she eyes me,
then gazes back to her animal world.

Change jangles in my pocket like broken glass.
This horse is all compulsive locomotion,
she pulls me under her wing,
in her I trust lemon sunlight,
the invisible grass,
the summoning song.

It is the most natural thing in the world
to depend on each other,
we work together,
we burn with forward movement,
we put away the dead.

This dark horse whispers art is not death,
it is temporary, miraculous escape from death:
a cat in the night under a leafless rose bush,
a calm, seated figure floating above
ripples of an otherwise still pond.

It is me,
knocked down,
breathless,
turning to the sight
of a thousand-pound horse
rushing the gate
and leaping over my head.

Her black, knobby knees contract and pump in my face,
like fists named danger and fear,
each trembling hair of her body vast yet finite,
as her hooves pass over me,
then drum survival.

Horses in Winter

Even now,
the cold front extends
its bear-like paw from Canada.

In its grasp
sounds splinter the clear blue air,
a frigid jet crackles above.

Horses stand in the weak mid-January sun,
one already shedding the hairs of a winter coat
as if he knows the sun's distant path towards spring.

I want to believe his russet brown hairs.

Horses do not slam their heads against desires,
they live in all forms of weather,
with hooves that cup the ice,
in clouds of foggy breath;
ice chunks cling to their muzzle hairs
and snow makes stiff blankets across their backs.

All this season I have contracted
like a moist ball of snow in someone else's mitten.

Yet this horse's winter coat pulls away,
a few hairs at a time
in my bare, cold palm.

THIS HORSE'S EARS

are warm red
russet,
black tips,
soft hairs dark inside.
With symmetry they curve outward,
swivel inward,
end in two alert points,
twin flames of hard listening.

Humans might long for a pentecost
with lathing tongues of fire;
this horse listens with fire,
his ears flicker at the sound:
a man chopping wood far away,
a rider breathing on his back,
a brown rabbit shivering under pines,
a miracle of listening.

This horse's ears of fire have soft fur
smoother than sable,
they glisten like mink,
know all forms of glossolalia.
Wise men bring gifts
to these ears,
and an apple.

The Wind Lightly Blows the Clouds Past the Sun

Large yellow stones wait silent by the water.
Pink and blue-gray stones
also wait.

Will there ever be
another world
like this one?

The light moves.
I bow my head
as it passes.

Where I Come from

My father was born in French River township
where small, north shore rivers—
Chester, Lester, Tischer, Amity—flow south
through juneberry, honeysuckle, and mossy rocks.

Now I sit beside an urban stream more canal than river,
an oily track of industry, utility, expedience.
I think French River must be wild,
it must have no footpaths.

But what do I know about terrain, the land, who my people are?
Did my people expect me to get drunk on Chardonnay
in a Polish bar with an Italian name
on the concrete bank of a late afternoon?

Stop talking to me now, put your lips and fingers on me,
put your blurry eyes on me.
Do you think this is the last error you will ever make?
This is a mouth, this, a river.

THROUGH THE ICE

Are you willing to suffer to feel good again?
You might try walking on thin ice,
you might try walking on slippery ice,
you might get hurt a little.
You might feel a little discomfort in this procedure.

You might give yourself two black eyes
and find yourself eyeless in Gaza
from watching someone fuck the cradle of civilization
or maybe you yourself will fuck the cradle of civilization.
It's cold in the holy land at Christmas time,
the little towns of Bethlehem, Gomorrah;
in Gaza, the air temp is 40 degrees,
they've blasted out the windows at Al Ahli hospital,
no slippery ice there,
but all the bodies super-cool.

When you find yourself in a long, narrow box,
feet pointing towards the east
(because we like to take our corpses straight
through the gate
to let the flying soul follow its lonely husk,
and we like the east, it smacks of resurrection,
we are an optimistic people,
we believe in souls),
if you follow a narrow box
to its logical conclusion,
you might find yourself among the sparrows.

But if you walk on ice and hear the heavy cracking sound,
if you walk on frozen water and fall through,
keep your clothes on,
they add buoyancy,
do not lose consciousness.

If you fall in,
fan out your scarf and parka
Ophelia-like,
turn in the direction you came
because it held you once,
place your arms on the unbroken surface of the lake and kick.

Ice can bridge an ocean and archipelagos,
ice will freeze the surface of your lake.
Ice will melt when atmosphere conditions are conducive
to water flowing freely.
Justice rolls like water,
righteousness like a mighty stream.
Words are not the antidote
but they might save you from drowning.

These words are not for melting.
The weight of something else is already breaking the ice,
fan out with everything you've got,
kick.

Fix My Shoes

The commercial on the screen says *you go girl*.
On this bar stool I am going to cross my legs,
and you are going to come right over here.
Help me with my shoes, honey,
because I am on the go-go-go.

I want to see that curly light brown hair on the very crown
                of your head.
I will overlook that cigarette clamped in the corner of your lips.
I will ignore that when your mouth opens I smell tooth decay.
Beer is fine for me.

Stoop down to fix my buckle, baby,
buy me a little drink.
Don't make me angry,
don't make me that one wheel on your car with the loosening
                lug nuts,
as if I'm making noise and you don't even know where it's
                coming from.

I've still got to take the little girl home.
Come on, sweetheart, fix my shoes.

A Life in Fairy Tales

The villagers are torching the bridges—
only the horse head

nailed to the field-gate
tells anyone the truth anymore.

One woman fights dirty for what she wants;
the daughter surrenders cambric squares

stained with her mother's own blood. They drift
down the river, one by one crying to her.

A bratty child falls into the swamp bed;
the marsh king crowns her queen of the underworld.

Nothing is left to the third son, so he has to improvise
and put his dead grandmother into the cart.

We are their offspring: loud, bent, glimmery by day,
silent, friendly, toadlike by night,

waiting for a rescuer to cut away the wolfskin
and find the shining child within.

It's hard to plan for this kind of future,
but in some situations, even the vegetables sing.

HUSH NOW

It's true,
sometimes mirror
rhymes with shiver.
On sing I, eternity through
and on sing I, on sing I,
eternity through and be joyful and sing.

Bar the glass,
close the windows and doors,
turn down the blinds, close the curtains.
That this is love wondrous. What.
Plates to dine on. Revenge.
Soul my own, soul my own.
This is love wondrous.

Open the cutlery drawer and set the table
for as many as will join the cold feast.
I'm free, I'm death from when
and on sing I, free.
I wish I knew what else to feed you.
What soul my own, soul my own?
What is this? Wondrous. Love.

Finnish Sauna

The weather has changed. Her belly is large.
She scrubs black soot off the sauna bench,
with six-year-old Irja helping. Her stomach squeezes.

Irja calls Papa, tells him to summon the midwife,
helps to heat the small house.
The sauna is smoking.

They let the smoke out, go in by the fire stones;
Äiti wants to be close to the heat,
the wood, fire, rocks, some water.

The midwife must be coming over an ocean.
The midwife is coming over the field with the wind;
she hurries up the little road.

Someone is coming, someone has spent
droplets of water over the stones.
They sing with hot moisture, their vapor rises.

Äiti draws pale steam into her mouth,
deep in her ribs. Or is she breathing it out?
The baby is coming out, out, out.

SPRUCE TREES AND BIRCH TREES

The small spruces fatten and grow taller
every year, they make flat land look softer.

I should have planted birches. I have to cross
the road, walk up the hill to find my medicine trees,

gather curled spring bark, trim boughs for switches.
What was it mother sang when she boiled bark?

Clear, clear. Birch steam smells like wet rope.
I bind together leaves the size of babies' fists,

leaves and branches fragrant with spring sap.
I'll steep the sticks in jars to make a tonic.

And what is spruce for? Pine tar, antiseptic,
famine bread. Sharp spears that last through winter.

Ridge Fire

When fire hits the pine it will explode.
All day hot winds have vented blazes
in the angry twilight of a smoke-filled sky.

Flames crest the hilltop of a world stone dry,
dirt cracks like flawed rock, grass withers,
aspens gray, their leaves like scraping paper.

It's not safe to lie in the swamp, it smolders
peat, it burns. A root cellar pocket
might feel cool till wildfire burns the door off.

Some chickens run to the cellar, they won't
burn, fire will just suck out all their air.
Now wind blows a billowing flame north,

toward someone else's farm,
and a woman crouches on Strand Road:
she tries to cover her baby from the flashover.

THE DANDELION GATHERER

Dandelion greens taste bitter
but their yellow pollen also has a flavor.

Each spring my finger tips turn gold
from deflowering their astringent sun-stroked tufts,
mashing them with water, sugar, lemon, tannin.

Do you like girls or boys?
It's a time-consuming process.

I was sorry one year when the yeast didn't take,
instead I had pretty liquid candy,
glassful after glassful with no kick.

Arvo's Farmhouse

There's no house there now, where Korkki Road curves,
its farm fields surrendered to thickets of popples and ash.

But here is his photo, Duluth, 1908.
He is 20, he wears a narrow wool suit, his fat tie is twisted.

He is always the younger brother, even at 60
when sister-in-law Mary drives to Duluth for his medicine.

He picks her dandelions for home-made wine in April,
he finds wild strawberries in hayfields in June.

He settles into a crease at the dead end of a road,
he farms potatoes, milks some cows, he picks what grows there.

He can walk up the gravel track to visit his older brother
and Mary, their daughters and sons. He drinks alone.

When Mary dies it's like the home well has run dry,
a chasm that needs to be capped and sealed with cement.

Arvo knows he's running out of his insulin,
he tilts the small bottle, swirling sediment into pale liquid.

He always knew this would happen. It's easier to stay home.
He has enough to drink. This house is his.

In Memory of Tennessee Williams, Who Died in 1983 After Choking on the Plastic Cap of a Pill Bottle

Lord, let me die a dignified death.
And Lord, let me die with my clothes on.

I understand it might not be my favorite outfit,
but Lord, I need to feel covered up a little.
Skirts and shirts drift up;
I must always wear underwear,
as we used to say, "Semper ubi sub ubi."

Lord, this means I can't die in bed,
even if it's winter, and I'm wearing a nightie,
those never stay put,
I toss and I turn and my hair frizzes up.
I'll have to find another way
to sleep
if I'm dying in bed.

My college roommate was like Sleeping Beauty,
she reclined supine,
hair outspread behind her,
arms straight at her sides.
Every time I sleep on my back
my throat dries out,
I gag.

I know I shouldn't eat in bed,
I could convulse on a sandwich like Mama Cass Elliot,
or heave and choke like Jimi Hendrix.
Lateral sleeping has its advantages;
I still have to do something about my hair.

And not in a bathroom, God, anything but that,
please do not pluck me from this mortal coil in that little room—
then there's the toilet,
though I'm sure it beats dying in an outhouse,
surely the fate of some of my ancestors.

Would it be so bad to die in a shower?
But there's Janet Leigh in "Psycho,"
and Elvis, maybe it's not just location,
maybe I'd like to be dressed and not split my seams.
Maybe I'd like to not choke,
at least not on something everyone knows
I should know not to put in my mouth!

God, not like Tennessee Williams,
so far from the kindness of strangers,
so tired of tapping the electrified fence between him
and his grandfather's church steeple.

Blanche DuBois could talk about God.
Maybe Tennessee's sister, Rose,
thought about God,
so quickly,
before her frontal lobotomy,
maybe Tennessee prayed
when he visited Rose, when he wrote that he loved her,
each day she gaped open her mouth for more pills,
six more decades until her heart gave out,
with a brain the doctors invaded with knives,
poking around,
feeling with steel for some type of reset button,
maybe.

For Olli Kiukkonen, Finnish Immigrant, Lynched in Duluth, Minnesota in 1918 Because He Did Not Enlist

Hold my hands and repeat after me,
right palm to right palm, left to left,
sing me an echo, turn at the antepenultimate sound,
chanting the words I intone, make the sounds continuous.

Sing me the story of Olli Kiukkonen,
ripped from his boarding house room, he just ached
to go home to *Suomi*, they broke down his door,
they grabbed him, they called themselves Knights of Liberty.

Angry he wasn't away at the warfront,
they called him a slacker and made the name stick with hot tar,
it made his skin boil. They called him a chicken,
dressed him in feathers, then found a rope,

slung its loose end on a fat sugar maple branch
near Lester Park, with its sparkling creek,
its stone bridge, not far from the picnic pavilion,
his screams in a language they smiled they didn't know.

When his body was found two weeks later, police
said he killed himself. No charges were filed.

*

*

Hold my hands, singing this song,
repeat his story, tell out the tragedy,
grieve this moment, breathe in, breathe out with me,
remember the man who just wants to go home.

WALKING THE LABYRINTH

The path is a series of loops, big and small—
I step forward, and forward, and forward,
listening to foot fall and the sound of feet treading,
and breathing, the measuring in and out,
and all of my muscles moving in slow, measured rhythm.
The hollowness and the wholeness of this routine movement,
the beauty of how at a turn one leg must move farther,
the stride of one leg reaching, overtaking another:
it astonishes me.

I see feet of others before and behind me
casting their own little pathways in varying patterns,
fanning out, closing in,
fanning out again, and then brought to a single line.
Who would have guessed that a spirit inhabits geometry?
I could measure cubic yards of air if I wanted to:
I am holding the air in my hands, palms tilted towards heaven.
It is full of oxygen.
It embraces me back.

To Change the World

First, I would give everyone a piano.

It is not enough to watch,
it is not enough to listen,
unless you are Keats
looking at the Elgin Marbles,
shocked by vividness,
light-headed from longing,
dreading mortal numbness,
the prickling static of a limb asleep,
trying to wake.

My body wakes. My hand begins to write,
my lips move, my fingers press piano keys,
the means to an end,
a way to open the body.

I want to sense the kindling in all things,
to join the whirling dancers on the stage,
their fuchsia turbans and fluttering silk scarves.
Those are my surprised pale hands
reaching toward the fevered poet—
that is my fear of death.

It is a flash of fire,
the hammer sound on steel-wound string,

and then the note,
reverberating.

QUANTUM LOVE

In all parallel universes,
parallel cities, parallel planets, parallel timelines,
                    parallel love affairs,
stretched like spaghetti,
we mingle intergenerationally:
I don't want to be in a foursome with DH Lawrence
but Katherine Mansfield I could shimmy with you!
Let's line up next to Dorothy Parker because
                    in this quantum universe,
Robert Benchley gets to go home with both of us
and also his wife who is simultaneously with
Fess Parker and Elizabeth I.

The Dalai Lama and Master Roshi are at this moment
                    meditating on
the explosive power of quantum love:
the war and fear committee declares it an act of terrorism
because in quantum love even the face of the enemy
will have at least temporary beauty.

With quantum love we'll vote for all political parties,
with quantum love we'll cherish all our children,
with quantum love we'll live in cities and in suburbs,
in mountains and in sea shells,

with quantum love we are never lonely,
with quantum love we embrace our solitude,
with quantum love we are all going home with each other,
with quantum love we are waking up together sideways,

with quantum love I am always saying hello to you,
hello, hello.

NOTES

"America Fever" is the name given to a movement of Finnish migration to America that swept that country from the 1880s to World War I. Much of it was driven by economic hardship in western Finland and also the dream of owning one's own farm.

"As We Drove" refers to the 1989 Loma Prieta earthquake in San Francisco. A two-level section of Interstate 880 collapsed on itself, killing 42 people.

"Bear Marriage" is a reimagining of an ancient Finnish tradition of revering and killing the bear. It involved elaborate rituals of singing, skiing to the bear's den, a formal feast, something akin to a marriage ceremony, and placing the bear's skull in a tall, sacred pine tree that faces the North Star. Similar bear traditions existed in several other ancient circumpolar cultures.

"For Olli Kiukkonen, Finnish Immigrant, Lynched in Duluth, Minnesota in 1918 Because He Did Not Enlist" refers to Finnish immigrant Olli Kiukkonen whose name is sometimes spelled "Kinkkonen," due to a misreading of a coroner's handwritten report. Little is known about his situation, but in September 1918, when nationalistic pro-war feelings were high and immigrants seen as potentially unpatriotic, a group of men calling themselves Knights of Liberty went to his boarding house in Duluth in the middle of the night and dragged him away. They wrote a letter to the *Duluth Herald* saying that they had tarred and feathered him for being a "slacker," i.e. someone who did not enlist in the military. His decomposed body was found a few weeks later, and it appeared he had been lynched. The Duluth police at the time, however, ruled it a suicide.

"Hush Now" contains rearranged words from the hymn "Wondrous Love." The lyrics are attributed to Alexander Means.

"New York, Carlton Arms Art Hotel" is an actual hotel in Manhattan. All of the rooms, bathrooms, hallways, stairways, etc. have been turned into paintings, sculptures, and art installations by various artists.

"Ridge Fire," refers to a group of fires October 10-12, 1918 that burned over 1500 square miles in northern Minnesota following a summer of drought. The fires spread quickly with high winds and killed more than 450 people.

"Spruce Trees and Birch Trees" mentions famine bread, also known as bark bread. Made from the membrane underneath the bark of a pine tree, it was labor-intensive and eaten in Finland during times of famine.

"Still Life" describes the famous painting by Edward Hopper, *Nighthawks*, in its first stanza.

"Through the Ice" contains references to the fighting between Israel and Palestine December 2008 to January 2009, shattering windows of Al Ahli Hospital in Gaza during the coldest months of the year and preventing aid workers and medical supplies from getting to wounded and dying innocent bystanders.

"Who Rules Your Heart?" contains a paraphrase from the poet George Herbert. His poetry was set to music by Ralph Vaughan Williams in the piece "Five Mystical Songs," the inspiration for this poem.

"Wish Hounds" is a term for spectral dogs of the Celtic Wild Hunt and other various folk tales of frightening dogs portending death or a near-escape from it. Other terms for spectral dog legends are Wisht Hounds, Yeth Hounds, Gabriel Hounds, Shucks, and Barghests. The best-known iteration of such phantom dog legends is Sir Arthur Conan Doyle's story, *The Hound of the Baskervilles*.

About the Author

LYNETTE REINI-GRANDELL has received grants for her work from the Finlandia Foundation and the Minnesota State Arts Board. Her poetry has been nominated for a Pushcart Prize and is part of a permanent art installation in room 5D of the Carlton Arms Hotel in Manhattan. She holds an MA and PhD in literature from the University of Minnesota, teaches at Normandale Community College, and has twice been president of the Minnesota Council of Teachers of English. A frequent performer of poetry, she appears regularly with the Bosso Poetry Company and co-hosts "Write on! Radio" on KFAI. She lives in Minneapolis with her husband, the transgender musician and multidisciplinary artist Venus de Mars, and regularly visits her horses, who live in a pasture. More information is available at her website, www.Reini-Grandell.com. *Approaching the Gate* is her first book.